YouTube Success

In 90 days

By Raphael Hudson

Copyright ©

TABLE OF CONTENT

1. Prologue of YouTube achievement

2. Setting Up your YouTube channel

3. Content Methodology: Tracking down Your Specialty

4. Making Top notch Recordings

5. Streamlining Video Titles, Portrayals, and Labels

6. Figuring out YouTube Investigation

7. Building Your Crowd through Website optimization

8. Adapting Your YouTube Channel

9. Drawing in with Your People group

10. Exploring YouTube's Arrangements and Rules

11. Growing your arrive at through cross-advancement

12. Sustaining Your Own Image

13. Upgrading Creation Quality

14. Utilizing Investigation for Development

15. Adaptation Methodologies and Then some

Introduction

YouTube Success in 3 Months is a comprehensive guide for aspiring YouTubers who want to achieve rapid growth and success on the platform. In today's digital age, YouTube has become a powerful tool for content creators to showcase their talents, share their expertise, and build a loyal community of followers.

In this book, you will discover proven strategies and techniques that will help you navigate the competitive landscape of YouTube and position yourself for success. Whether you're a beginner or have already started your YouTube journey, this book will provide you with invaluable insights and practical tips to take your channel to the next level.

With step-by-step instructions, real-life examples, and expert advice, you will learn how to set up your YouTube channel, create compelling content, optimize your videos for maximum visibility, engage with your audience, monetize your channel, and much more. By implementing the strategies outlined in this book, you will be well-equipped to achieve YouTube success in just three months.

Chapter 1

Prologue to YouTube Achievement

In the principal section of "YouTube Progress in 90 days," we dig into the gigantic power and open doors that YouTube offers to content makers. We investigate the ascent of YouTube as a main stage for video utilization, with billions of clients watching recordings consistently.

This part sets the establishment for your YouTube venture, assisting you with understanding the possible effect and arrive at your channel can have. We talk about the different specialties and kinds that flourish with YouTube and how you can recognize the one that lines up with your interests and mastery.

Moreover, we feature the significance of objective setting and fostering a reasonable vision for your YouTube channel. We guide you through the most common way of characterizing your main interest group and understanding their necessities and inclinations, guaranteeing that your substance impacts them actually.

Toward the finish of Part 1, you will have a strong comprehension of why YouTube is a stage worth putting your significant investment into. You will be spurred to leave on your excursion towards YouTube achievement and anxious to gain proficiency with the techniques that will be canvassed in the ensuing sections.

CHAPTER 2

Setting Up Your YouTube Channel

YouTube success in 90 days, we plunge into the down to earth steps of setting up your YouTube channel. We comprehend that beginning can be overpowering, however with our direction, you'll have your divert going in a matter of moments.

We start by making sense of the significance of picking a convincing channel name that mirrors your substance and reverberates with your ideal interest group. We give tips on conceptualizing inventive and important names that are not difficult to articulate and look for on YouTube.

Then, we walk you through the method involved with making an appealing channel logo and flag. Your visual marking assumes a significant part in catching watchers' consideration and laying out your channel's personality. We share configuration tips and suggest apparatuses that can assist you with making proficient looking illustrations regardless of whether you have visual computerization experience.

When your visual marking is set up, we guide you through the means of advancing your channel's About area. This is a potential chance to present yourself, share your channel's motivation, and give connects to your virtual entertainment records or site. We examine viable composing procedures to make your About segment connecting with and influential.

Moreover, we clarify how for set up your channel's highlighted video and arrange your playlists. These components add to a positive client experience, making it simpler for watchers to explore your substance and find a greater amount of what you bring to the table.

In conclusion, we cover the specialized parts of setting up your channel, for example, connecting your YouTube channel to a Google account, changing protection settings, and modifying your channel's URL. We give bit by bit directions and investigate normal issues that new YouTubers might experience during the arrangement cycle.

Toward the finish of Part 2, you will have a completely improved YouTube channel that is outwardly engaging, very much organized, and prepared to grandstand your substance to the world. You will have acquired the important information to explore the arrangement cycle effortlessly, setting areas of strength for a for your YouTube achievement venture.

CHAPTER 3

Content Methodology: Tracking down Your Specialty

In Chapter 3 of "YouTube Progress in 90 days," we dig into the significance of fostering a substance methodology and tracking down your specialty on YouTube. Understanding your ideal interest group and conveying content that impacts them is vital to building an unwavering endorser base.

We start by examining the idea of a specialty and why it is significant to distinguish one for your YouTube channel. Reducing your center permits you to situate yourself as a specialist in a particular region and draw in watchers who are really keen on your substance.

We guide you through the method involved with directing statistical surveying to recognize famous specialties and evaluate their true capacity for development. We give tips on utilizing YouTube search and catchphrase research devices to find moving points and watchwords connected with your specialty.

Whenever you have recognized your specialty, we assist you with characterizing your substance points of support — the center subjects or topics that will shape the foundation of your channel. We accentuate the significance of consistency and legitimacy in conveying content that lines up with your specialty and resounds with your interest group.

Moreover, we investigate different substance configurations and assist you with deciding the most appropriate ones for your specialty. Whether it's instructional exercises, video blogs, audits, or amusement, we give experiences into the qualities and contemplations of each configuration, assisting you with pursuing an educated choice.

Moreover, we examine the meaning of narrating in drawing in your crowd and making an association. We give narrating procedures that can raise your substance and make it seriously convincing, expanding watcher commitment and maintenance.

Toward the finish of Section 3, you will have a reasonable comprehension of your specialty, content points of support, and the kinds of content you will make. You will be outfitted with the information and systems to foster a substance technique that reverberates with your interest group, making way for your YouTube achievement.

CHAPTER 4

Making Top notch Recordings

In Chapter 4 of "YouTube Outcome in 90 days," we investigate the significant part of making excellent recordings that charm and draw in your crowd. With the right strategies and devices, you can raise the creation worth of your substance and hang out in the packed YouTube scene.

We start by examining the significance of arranging your recordings prior to raising a ruckus around town button. We guide you through the most common way of making a diagram or content, deciding the central issues you need to cover, and coordinating your substance in a consistent and drawing in way.

Then, we dig into the specialized parts of video creation. We cover fundamental hardware, like cameras, mouthpieces, and lighting arrangements, and give suggestions in view of your financial plan and explicit requirements. We additionally examine the significance of sound quality and give tips on catching clear and fresh sound.

Also, we investigate different shooting strategies, including outlining, creation, and camera development, to add visual premium to your recordings. We examine the standard of thirds, the significance of legitimate lighting, and how to make an outwardly satisfying foundation that upgrades your substance.

Moreover, we give direction on altering your recordings utilizing famous altering programming. We make sense of the fundamental altering procedures, like managing, changes, and adding overlays or text, to upgrade the stream and visual allure of your substance. We likewise stress the significance of keeping a reliable altering style to lay out your channel's visual personality.

Besides, we talk about the meaning of thumbnails and video titles in drawing in watchers to tap on your recordings. We give tips on making eye-getting thumbnails that precisely address your substance and utilizing convincing titles that arouse interest and advance accessibility.

Toward the finish of Part 4, you will have a strong comprehension of the specialized and innovative parts of making excellent recordings. You will be outfitted with the information and abilities to plan, shoot, and alter recordings that feature your substance expertly, spellbinding your crowd and expanding your possibilities of YouTube achievement.

CHAPTER 5

Streamlining Video Titles, Portrayals, and Labels

In Chapter 5 of "YouTube Outcome in 90 days," we plunge into the specialty of streamlining your video titles, depictions, and labels to augment perceivability and reach on YouTube. Successful advancement methods can altogether help your video's possibilities being found by the right crowd.

We start by making sense of the significance of catchphrase examination and how it assumes a crucial part in enhancing your recordings for search. We present different watchword research instruments and strategies that can assist you with distinguishing pertinent catchphrases and expressions that line up with your substance and have critical hunt volume.

Then, we guide you through the method involved with creating eye catching video titles. We examine the force of utilizing catchphrases decisively in your titles while keeping a convincing and interactive organization. We additionally give tips on consolidating interest, desperation, and pertinence to tempt watchers to snap and watch your recordings.

Moreover, we investigate the streamlining of video portrayals. We talk about the ideal length, construction, and utilization of catchphrases inside your portrayals to give important data to the two watchers and search calculations. We additionally underscore the significance of including applicable connections, timestamps, and invitations to take action to improve watcher commitment and collaboration.

Furthermore, we dig into the universe of video labels. We make sense of how labels add to's how YouTube might interpret your substance and assist it with prescribing your recordings to the right crowd. We give procedures to choosing suitable labels that precisely address your video and supplement your picked watchwords.

In addition, we examine the significance of video thumbnails and what they mean for navigate rates. We give tips on making outwardly engaging and tempting thumbnails that mirror the substance of your video and allure watchers to snap and watch.

Toward the finish of Part 5, you will have a far reaching comprehension of how to upgrade your video titles, depictions, labels, and thumbnails to increment perceivability, draw in the right crowd, and work on your video's

 chances of positioning higher in list items. You will be furnished with the information and methods to improve your recordings really, setting major areas of strength for a for YouTube achievement.

CHAPTER 6

Figuring out YouTube Investigation

In Part 6 of "YouTube Outcome in 90 days," we dive into the domain of YouTube examination and the significant bits of knowledge it accommodates enhancing your channel's exhibition. By grasping your crowd, their way of behaving, and the measurements that matter, you can pursue information driven choices to fuel your YouTube achievement.

We start by acquainting you with YouTube's examination dashboard and making sense of the key measurements you ought to zero in on. From perspectives and watch time to commitment measurements like likes, remarks, and offers, we assist you with understanding the meaning of every data of interest and how it mirrors your channel's exhibition.

Then, we investigate the Crowd tab in YouTube Examination, which gives important segment data about your watchers. We examine how to break down your crowd's age, orientation, area, and interests to acquire experiences into who your substance is resounding with. This information assists you with fitting your substance to more readily serve your main interest group's inclinations.

Besides, we jump into the Arrive at tab, which offers bits of knowledge into how watchers find your substance. We investigate the wellsprings of traffic, including YouTube search, proposed recordings, outside references, and that's only the tip of the iceberg. By understanding how watchers find your recordings, you can improve your substance and advancement procedures to contact a more extensive crowd.

Moreover, we examine the Watch Time tab, which gives definite data about how long watchers watch your recordings. We dig into measurements like normal view term, crowd maintenance, and playback areas to recognize examples and regions for development. By making connecting with and convincing substance that holds watchers' consideration, you can increment watch time and work on your channel's presentation.

Also, we investigate the Commitment tab, which features the degree of watcher collaboration with your substance. We analyze measurements like preferences, remarks, offers, and supporter development to check crowd commitment and dedication. By empowering dynamic commitment and encouraging a feeling of local area, you can develop a devoted fan base that upholds your channel's development.

Toward the finish of Section 6, you will have an exhaustive comprehension of YouTube Examination and its job in streamlining your channel's exhibition. You will actually want to decipher the information, distinguish patterns, and go with information driven choices to improve your substance system, draw in your crowd, and drive your YouTube achievement.

CHAPTER 7

Building Your Crowd through Website optimization

In Section 7 of "YouTube Progress in 90 days," we investigate the force of Site improvement (Search engine optimization) in building your YouTube crowd. By improving your recordings and channel for search, you can increment perceivability, draw in important watchers, and develop your endorser base.

We start by making sense of the essentials of YouTube Search engine optimization. We examine the job of catchphrases in positioning your recordings in list items and give techniques to leading watchword research. By distinguishing high-traffic and low-rivalry watchwords, you can advance your video titles, depictions, labels, and records to further develop search rankings.

Then, we dive into the significance of video metadata. We talk about how to compose convincing and catchphrase rich video titles, portrayals, and labels that precisely address your substance and tempt watchers to click. We additionally accentuate the meaning of remembering important watchwords for your video records to upgrade accessibility.

Besides, we investigate the force of playlists in helping your channel's Web optimization. We examine how arranging your recordings into themed playlists assists YouTube with understanding your substance better and builds the possibilities of your recordings being suggested. We give tips on making enhanced playlist titles, portrayals, and plans that benefit the two watchers and search calculations.

Furthermore, we talk about the job of video thumbnails in drawing in clicks from query items. We give systems to making outwardly engaging and important thumbnails that stick out and allure watchers to pick your video over others. We likewise stress the significance of keeping up with consistency in thumbnail plan to lay out memorability.

Additionally, we investigate the meaning of client commitment signals in Search engine optimization. We talk about how measurements like watch time, active clicking factor (CTR), and

crowd maintenance impact search rankings. By making drawing in and excellent substance that resounds with your crowd, you can work on these measurements and indicate to YouTube that your recordings are important and meriting higher rankings.

Toward the finish of Section 7, you will have a complete comprehension of YouTube Search engine optimization and its job in building your crowd. You will be outfitted with the information and methods to enhance your recordings, channel, playlists, and thumbnails to increment perceivability, draw in pertinent watchers, and drive your YouTube accomplishment forward.

CHAPTER 8

Adapting Your YouTube Channel

In Section 8 of "YouTube Outcome in 90 days," we investigate the thrilling domain of adapting your YouTube channel and transforming your enthusiasm into a type of revenue. We guide you through the most common way of opening different adaptation includes and amplifying your acquiring potential on YouTube.

We start by talking about the YouTube Accomplice Program (YPP) and the prerequisites for qualification. We make sense of the significance of arriving at the base edges of 1,000 supporters and 4,000 watch hours in the beyond a year. We give techniques to developing your supporter base and expanding watch time to meet these necessities and get to adaptation highlights.

Then, we dive into the various ways you can adapt your channel. We examine the YouTube Accomplice Program's essential income transfer, which is through advertisements shown on your recordings. We give bits of knowledge into promotion designs, promotion arrangement methodologies, and streamlining your substance for higher promotion income.

Besides, we investigate extra income transfers accessible to YouTubers. We talk about the YouTube Premium income share, channel participations, stock rack joining, and Super Visit and Super Stickers. We make sense of how these elements work, how to empower them on your channel, and methodologies for amplifying your income through these roads.

Also, we dig into brand organizations and sponsorships. We give direction on the most proficient method to recognize and move toward potential brand coordinated efforts, arrange bargains, and keep up with valid organizations that line up with your channel's substance and values. We examine the significance of keeping up with straightforwardness and divulgence to guarantee a dependable connection with your crowd.

Besides, we talk about the meaning of broadening your revenue transfers past YouTube. We investigate open doors, for example, associate promoting, selling computerized items or courses, crowdfunding stages, and brand supports. By utilizing these outer roads, you can make numerous income streams and improve your procuring potential as a substance maker.

Toward the finish of Part 8, you will have a complete comprehension of how to adapt your YouTube channel successfully. You will be furnished with the information and techniques to open adaptation highlights, improve your substance for higher promotion income, investigate extra income streams, and fabricate a reasonable pay from your YouTube channel.

CHAPTER 9

Drawing in with Your People group

In Section 9 of "YouTube Outcome in 90 days," we dive into the significance of drawing in with your local area and building areas of strength for a with your watchers. Cultivating a dedicated and dynamic local area around your channel is indispensable for long haul accomplishment on YouTube.

We start by talking about the meaning of crowd association and commitment. We investigate the different ways you can draw in with your local area, for example, answering remarks, requesting criticism and ideas, and facilitating live streams or round table discussions. We give tips on making an inviting and comprehensive environment where watchers feel esteemed and heard.

Then, we dive into the force of remarks and how to successfully oversee them. We talk about techniques for directing and answering remarks, managing negative or malicious remarks, and cultivating significant conversations inside your local area. We likewise stress the significance of setting clear local area rules to keep a conscious and steady climate.

Moreover, we investigate the advantages of facilitating live streams and associating with your watchers continuously. We give direction on arranging and advancing live streams, drawing in with your crowd during the stream, and utilizing live talks and intuitive elements to make a vivid encounter. We likewise examine the worth of joint efforts and co-facilitating live streams with different makers to grow your scope and draw in with new crowds.

Moreover, we talk about the job of virtual entertainment in local area commitment. We investigate different virtual entertainment stages and how they can supplement your YouTube channel. We give techniques to utilizing stages like Twitter, Instagram, and Facebook to associate with your crowd, share in the background content, and advance your recordings.

Additionally, we dig into the significance of crowd input and utilizing it to work on your content. We examine the worth of examination, surveys, and reviews in figuring out your crowd's inclinations and fitting your substance to their requirements. We likewise underline the meaning of persistently developing and adjusting your substance in light of criticism to keep up with crowd interest and dedication.

Toward the finish of Section 9, you will have an extensive comprehension of how to draw in with your local area and cultivate areas of strength for a with your watchers. You will be furnished with the information and techniques to establish an inviting and intuitive climate, oversee remarks really, have connecting live streams, influence virtual entertainment, and consolidate crowd input to sustain a flourishing YouTube people group.

CHAPTER 10

Exploring YouTube's Arrangements and Rules

In Part 10 of "YouTube Outcome in 90 days," we plunge into the significance of understanding and exploring YouTube's arrangements and rules. As a substance maker, it is pivotal to comply to these principles to guarantee the life span and outcome of your channel.

We start by giving an outline of YouTube's People group Rules. We make sense of the kinds of content that are denied or limited on the stage, like disdain discourse, savagery, provocation, and copyright encroachment. We underscore the significance of making content that consents to these rules to keep a positive and safe climate for your crowd.

Then, we dig into copyright and fair use arrangements. We talk about the significance of regarding protected innovation freedoms and give direction on the most proficient method to keep away from copyright strikes. We investigate the idea of fair use and give instances of when involving protected material in your content is adequate.

Besides, we investigate YouTube's adaptation approaches and the qualification prerequisites for adaptation highlights. We examine the sorts of content that might be demonetized or restricted regarding promotion income. We give techniques to making publicist agreeable substance and staying away from content that might disregard these arrangements.

Furthermore, we talk about the job of YouTube's calculation and what it means for video suggestions and perceivability. We investigate the idea of "misleading content" and examine the significance of making fair and drawing in happy that lines up with watcher assumptions. We likewise give tips on streamlining your substance to expand its possibilities being suggested by the calculation.

Also, we dive into the strategies and rules with respect to paid advancements, sponsorships, and supports. We talk about the significance of straightforwardness and divulgence while working together with brands or advancing items. We give direction on the best way to appropriately uncover supported content to keep up with trust and straightforwardness with your crowd.

Toward the finish of Part 10, you will have a complete comprehension of YouTube's strategies and rules. You will be furnished with the information and systems to explore these principles, make content that conforms with YouTube's rules, stay away from copyright issues, comply to adaptation strategies, and keep up with straightforwardness and entrust with your crowd.

CHAPTER 11

Growing your arrive at through cross-advancement

in part 11 of "youtube outcome in 90 days," we investigate the force of cross-advancement and cooperation to extend your scope and become your youtube channel. by combining efforts with different makers and utilizing various stages, you can take advantage of new crowds and speed up your channel's development.

we start by examining the advantages of cooperation and the various kinds of coordinated efforts you can participate in. we investigate the potential outcomes of co-making recordings, highlighting each other in satisfied, or facilitating joint occasions. we give systems to distinguishing possible teammates and contacting them in an expert and commonly valuable way.

then, we dig into the idea of cross-advancement and how it can help both you and your teammate. we talk about the significance of choosing associates whose content lines up with yours and whose crowd has comparative interests. we give tips on advancing each other's channels and content through yell outs, video comments, and virtual entertainment cross-advancement.

besides, we investigate the job of visitor appearances and meetings in growing your range. we examine the benefit of being a visitor on different channels or digital recordings and how it opens you to new crowds. we give direction on tracking down open doors to visitor appearances and utilizing them to feature your mastery and fabricate your power inside your specialty.

furthermore, we talk about the force of utilizing virtual entertainment stages to cross-advance your youtube channel. we investigate procedures for using stages like instagram, twitter, facebook, and tiktok to share mysteries, in the background content, and features from your recordings. we underline the significance of guiding your online entertainment devotees to your youtube channel to drive traffic and increment supporters.

also, we dive into the idea of making content for different stages to draw in new watchers to your youtube channel. we examine the potential outcomes of making short-structure recordings, mysteries, or selective substance for stages like instagram reels or tiktok. we give tips on streamlining these recordings to provoke watchers' curiosity and lead them to your fundamental youtube channel.

toward the finish of section 11, you will have an extensive comprehension of cross-advancement and cooperation systems to extend your range. you will be furnished with the information and methods to recognize likely teammates, take part in cross-advancement, influence visitor appearances, use online entertainment stages, and make content for different stages to draw in new watchers and speed up your youtube channel's development.

CHAPTER 12

Sustaining Your Own Image

In Part 12 of "YouTube Progress in 90 days," we dig into the significance of supporting your own image as a substance maker. Building areas of strength for a genuine brand character not just assists you with hanging out in a packed space yet in addition makes an enduring association with your crowd.

We start by examining the idea of individual marking and its importance in the advanced scene. We investigate the components that add to a convincing individual brand, like your interesting character, values, and narrating style. We give direction on distinguishing your assets, interests, and subject matters to actually shape your own image.

Then, we dig into characterizing your main interest group and grasping their necessities and inclinations. We examine the significance of crowd exploration and how it assists you with fitting your substance to resound with your watchers. We give systems to directing overviews, investigating crowd socioeconomics, and looking for criticism to acquire experiences into your main interest group's inspirations and wants.

Moreover, we investigate the job of consistency in building major areas of strength for a brand. We examine the significance of keeping a predictable tone, visual style, and informing across your substance, thumbnails, channel workmanship, and online entertainment presence. We give tips on making a durable brand character that mirrors your qualities and draws in your ideal crowd.

Moreover, we talk about the force of narrating in private marking. We investigate how convincing narrating can enthrall your crowd, encourage profound associations, and make your substance critical. We give procedures to making connecting with accounts and utilizing narrating components to make effective and shareable substance.

In addition, we dig into the meaning of legitimacy and straightforwardness in private marking. We talk about the significance of being certifiable, legit, and interesting to fabricate entrust with your crowd. We give systems to sharing individual stories, examples, and difficulties that reverberate with your watchers and make a feeling of local area.

Toward the finish of Section 12, you will have a far reaching comprehension of supporting your own image as a substance maker. You will be furnished with the information and systems to characterize your own image, figure out your interest group, keep up with consistency, influence narrating, and develop realness to make areas of strength for a charming individual brand that resounds with your crowd and drives your YouTube achievement.

CHAPTER 13

Upgrading Creation Quality

In Section 13 of "YouTube Outcome in 90 days," we investigate the significance of improving your creation quality to make proficient and outwardly engaging recordings that spellbind your crowd. By working on the specialized parts of your substance, you can hoist the general review insight and draw in additional watchers to your channel.

We start by talking about the meaning of video and sound quality. We investigate the significance of putting resources into a decent camera, lighting gear, and sound recording gadgets to catch high-goal recordings with clear sound. We give tips on picking the right gear acceptable for you and streamlining your shooting climate for ideal outcomes.

Then, we dig into the craft of video altering. We examine the job of altering in upgrading the stream, pacing, and narrating of your recordings. We give experiences into famous video altering programming and procedures for managing, cutting, adding changes, and consolidating special visualizations to make outwardly captivating and cleaned content.

Moreover, we investigate the significance of making outwardly engaging thumbnails and channel craftsmanship. We talk about the effect of convincing thumbnails in drawing in watchers and expanding navigate rates. We give tips on planning eye-getting thumbnails that precisely address your substance and allure watchers to snap and watch your recordings. Moreover, we examine the significance of reliable marking and visual style in channel workmanship to make a firm and expert appearance.

Moreover, we talk about the job of illustrations and livelinesss in upgrading your recordings. We investigate procedures for integrating lower thirds, text overlays, and livelinesss to add visual premium and pass on data successfully. We likewise examine the utilization of movement illustrations, introduction/outro successions, and end screens to make an essential and firm review insight.

Also, we dive into the significance of advancing your recordings for various stages and gadgets. We talk about the meaning of making versatile substance and guaranteeing that your recordings are open and agreeable across different gadgets. We give tips on enhancing video designs, angle proportions, and subtitles to take care of various survey inclinations and boost reach.

Toward the finish of Section 13, you will have a thorough comprehension of how to improve your creation quality and make outwardly engaging recordings. You will be furnished with the information and methods to further develop video and sound quality, ace video altering, plan enthralling thumbnails and channel craftsmanship, integrate illustrations and movements, and advance your recordings for various stages and gadgets. Lifting your creation quality will assist you with hanging out in the YouTube scene and draw in a bigger crowd to your channel.

CHAPTER 14

Utilizing Investigation for Development

In Section 14 of "YouTube Outcome in 90 days," we investigate the force of examination and information driven bits of knowledge in energizing the development of your YouTube channel. By getting it and utilizing the measurements and information given by YouTube, you can pursue informed choices and streamline your substance procedure to drive commitment and increment your scope.

We start by talking about the significance of YouTube Investigation and the vital measurements to zero in on. We dig into measurements, for example, watch time, crowd maintenance, navigate rates, and supporter development. We give direction on deciphering these measurements to acquire experiences into watcher conduct, recognize patterns, and measure the exhibition of your recordings.

Then, we investigate the worth of crowd socioeconomics and how they can illuminate your substance procedure. We examine the significance of figuring out your watchers' age, orientation, area, and interests to fit your substance to their inclinations. We give methodologies to leading crowd reviews, breaking down socioeconomics information, and utilizing this data to make content that reverberates with your ideal interest group.

Moreover, we dig into the idea of content execution examination. We examine methods for dissecting the presentation of individual recordings, recognizing examples of accomplishment, and understanding the reason why certain recordings perform better compared to other people. We give bits of knowledge into the effect of variables like video length, content configuration, and thumbnail plan on watcher commitment.

Furthermore, we investigate the job of Website design enhancement (Site improvement) in further developing your video discoverability. We examine the significance of streamlining your video titles, portrayals, labels, and thumbnails to rank higher in query items and proposals. We give tips on directing catchphrase research, utilizing moving themes, and enhancing your metadata to draw in additional watchers to your recordings.

Additionally, we dig into the force of trial and error and A/B testing in refining your substance technique. We talk about the advantages of attempting various organizations, styles, and subjects to check crowd reaction and emphasize on your substance. We give systems to directing controlled tests, estimating their effect, and integrating the bits of knowledge acquired into your future substance creation.

Toward the finish of Section 14, you will have a complete comprehension of how to use investigation and information driven bits of knowledge to drive the development of your YouTube channel. You will be furnished with the information and procedures to decipher YouTube Examination measurements, dissect crowd socioeconomics, measure content execution, advance your recordings for search, and trial with various substance draws near. By saddling the force of information, you can pursue informed choices and constantly work on your substance system to make long haul progress on YouTube.

CHAPTER 15

Adaptation Methodologies and Then some

In Part 15 of "YouTube Outcome in 90 days," we investigate adaptation methodologies and extra roads to produce pay from your YouTube channel. While making drawing in happy is fundamental, adapting your channel can give a feasible wellspring of income and backing your development as a substance maker.

We start by examining the prerequisites and interaction for joining the YouTube Accomplice Program. We investigate the rules for qualification, for example, watch hours and endorser count, and give direction on the most proficient method to meet these prerequisites. We likewise examine the advantages of turning into a YouTube Accomplice, including admittance to adaptation highlights like promotions, channel participations, and Super Talk.

Then, we dive into the different adaptation choices accessible to content makers. We examine the significance of broadening your income streams to limit dependence on a solitary source. We investigate choices like brand organizations, supported content, stock deals, and crowdfunding stages. We give bits of knowledge into how to distinguish reasonable brand coordinated efforts, arrange arrangements, and influence your impact to make commonly advantageous associations.

Besides, we examine the meaning of making and offering product to your crowd. We investigate methodologies for planning and advancing marked stock that lines up with your own image and resounds with your watchers. We give tips on utilizing stages like Teespring or Print-on-Request administrations to make and sell your product with negligible forthright expenses.

Also, we investigate the idea of crowdfunding and how it can uphold your substance creation endeavors. We examine stages like Patreon, Ko-fi, or Kickstarter that permit your watchers to contribute monetarily to your channel. We give experiences into making convincing compensations for your allies and sustaining an unwavering local area of benefactors.

Besides, we dig into the significance of building major areas of strength for a rundown and using email showcasing to draw in with your crowd and advance your substance and items. We talk about procedures for catching email addresses, making significant bulletins, and utilizing email computerization to support your endorser base and drive transformations.

Moreover, we talk about the capability of fanning out past YouTube and investigating extra stages and income streams. We investigate choices, for example, podcasting, public talking commitment, online courses, or making advanced items like digital books or layouts. We give bits of knowledge into how to use your ability and crowd to investigate these valuable open doors and produce pay beyond YouTube.

Toward the finish of Part 15, you will have an exhaustive comprehension of adaptation techniques and extra roads to produce pay from your YouTube channel. You will be outfitted with the information and systems to join the YouTube Accomplice Program, investigate brand associations and supported content, make and sell stock, use crowdfunding stages, influence email advertising, and investigate extra income streams. Adapting your channel successfully will furnish you with the monetary strength to keep making quality substance and seek after your energy as a substance maker.